This page is intentionaly left blank.

*Truth is*

**© 2023 KD Gates**

All rights reserved. No part of this publication may be reproduced, stored in a retrieval system or transmitted in any form or by any means, electronic, mechanical, photocopying, recording or otherwise without the prior permission of the publisher or in accordance with the provisions of the Copyright, Designs and Patents Act 1988 or under the terms of any licence permitting limited copying issued by the Copyright Licensing Agency.

**Typesetting and Cover Design:** Pentip Press

**Library of Congress Control Number:**

**ISBN-13:** 979-8-9852433-6-9

# Warning!

Bold truths for brave souls ahead.

> "The lies we tell ourselves are the lies most people tell themselves. At some point, we've got to teach one another the truth."

I'm forever seduced and bound by that quote, as truth-telling to a fault puts you at fault for being authentic. Yet, I'll never forget the words of my late mother—"Speak truth or speak nothing at all," she'd say. And her mantra, wise before my time, remains deeply etched in my mind today.

Mentally and ungrudgingly, I've learned to appreciate and embody her proverb. Like a soul to a corpse, I live, love, and breathe proverbial sense into dead vowels and syllables—into words heard by some and disliked by many.

Since then, being an oracle of sincerity, I've jotted countless proverbs in journals, posted them in social spaces, and written them in books. Some I've hung on walls and sold as posters, too. Where I go, they follow as I unapologetically paint the world any other color but Fake.

Coloring outside the lines, candidly tattooing hope on the hopeless, and healing on the hurting, I often remind myself and ask others to remember that we live in a world that encourages us to mask our truths, to paint over them with fairytales and socially acceptable facades. I urge them to embrace reality and entertain the theory of what if. What if rather than rose-red, we painted the world Real and, instead of seeking a temporary place to escape, we discover a permanent place to rest? Would you dare leave Wonderland for Freedom?

All hail to brutal honesty; most of us would say no. Because, like the quote above, embracing these hard, raw, and uncomfortable truths is hard, raw, and uncomfortable. But, the key to understanding ourselves and the world around us rests not in comfort but in discomfort. And this book, not meant to provide a comforting escape, presents a promising start.

Truth Is, refreshingly blunt, serves as a mirror reflecting the clear-cut realities of life. It's an exploration into the depths of the human condition, a deep dive into the choppy waters we seldom dare to swim. After all, "Some truths are like shards of glass under our feet—painful when stepped on, yet distinctly beautiful when held up to the light."

And even darkness, unlit and secretly cowardly, longs for the light.

Even darkness, the purveyor of deception and half-truths, finds no white lies in the underbelly of whitespace, just harsh realities and epiphanies to enlighten you. Just secrets, page after page, peeling back another layer of the human experience, revealing truths as profound as they are disconcerting and an eye-opening journey as challenging as it is worthwhile—I promise.

Remember, the goal of this book is not to bring you down but to uplift you—to help you reframe your perspective and find strength, wisdom, and understanding amid life's trials. By diving headfirst into these brutal truths, we can have a greater appreciation for life and a deeper understanding of ourselves.

So, if you're ready to face the truth? If you're willing to step into the light, however harsh it may be, and see yourself and the world around you with unflinching honesty, turn the page. A journey of discovery, growth, and awareness awaits.

Read it without regret.

Half-truths are whole lies.

Feeling lost and feeling lonely are real feelings we all feel. Don't let the cravings of a warm body drive you back to a cold heart. #relatable

People pretend to be something they are not all the time. The key, however, is to be authentic so you won't need to.

Truth is, the push, the pull was your love story. Yes, it was short-lived, but it was still your story.

Doing it scared is something you will have to do—eventually.

Doubt, like Fear, shows up when you are walking the right path. Keep going.

If you must think about it,

the answer is no until it's

a firm yes.

They will blame you because you told them to go right, and they chose to go left. Keep walking forward.

Forcing yourself to love someone is not real love; it's forced affection. It will not last.

When it comes to love, you may never know the "why" behind the breakup. This lack of clarity will leave you feeling broken. Cry, wonder why, and cry some more. Then, pick up the pieces and move on.

Most religions are manufactured and somewhat fictional. It's the relationship between you and God that's real—that matters.

Most souls are sheep, too lazy to lead. Don't become a sheep to belong to the herd.

Some people fear positive power, so they will do every negative thing they can to make you feel powerless.

Although it does not feel like it initially, stepping away from toxicity to find peace is a healthy move.

Love hurts sometimes. Most times, love is confusing. But clarity does come.

Time moves fast, but life moves faster. Keep up, but don't race.
Pace yourself.

Everyone makes mistakes, but not everyone admits to their mistake making. Yet, they will hold you accountable for your mistakes but won't take accountability for theirs. #fyi

Somebody will make you
the villain in their story.
But you can be
the hero in yours.

Developing feelings after intimacy is natural, and oxytocin is to blame. But don't blame or shame yourself for responding naturally. And don't let them blame or shame you either.
#attachment

Life deals us many hands—some good, some bad. Yet, the hand we choose to hold is how our lives will go.

There is evil in this world, and a part of it lives within. But goodness lives there, too. The side you choose is up to you.

You will never be good enough for those who don't feel good enough for themselves. Remember that.

People know when you're lying.
Stop fooling yourself.

Fake is favored. Real is ridiculed. Be authentic, anyway.

Most enemies hide in plain sight. They're insects, sap-sucking infestations seeking to feed on your energy. Stay watchful.

Everyone appearing to be an enemy is not always an enemy. Everyone presenting themselves as an ally is not always an ally.

It is never too late for positive change, but your mind will say otherwise. Don't listen.

Being yourself is better than trying to be someone else. It's dangerous trying to fit a skin you've never been in.

Depression is real.

The choice to overcome it

is just as real.

There is death, and there is life. We cannot have one without the other.

You will ask questions, but the answers you crave will not come. Instead, your answers will come when you stop seeking and start living.

Sometimes,

the happy ending ends.

Write a new story with a

happier ending.

The friendships you thought would last forever may have expiration dates.

Loyalty will keep you in disloyal situations. Knowing when to go is the first step, and leaving is the second.

People will choose money over love and sex over genuine connection. They will stab you in the back and betray you, too. These are not your people.

Sometimes lust feels better—no strings attached. Yet, these cravings don't last, and the feelings don't either. Choose love.

Although it is easier to avoid taking responsibility, sometimes it is your fault. Therefore, take accountability.

Your generational curses are broken. Rather than focusing on putting the pieces together, focus on staying whole.

Most masks are worn by people you grow to love and trust.

The cheating, the forgiving, the cheating again continues because, yes, you forgave them, but you forgot to leave.

Relatives can be strangers and even stranger relatives.

That deep thought may have a deeper meaning. Pay attention and listen.
#intuition

You were the best candidate for the position—their insecurity told them otherwise.

Most of the time, a stranger will support you before those closest to you. It's not personal; it's proof. Proof that you can and will conquer your goals and crush success.

Love is not always generous. Some love is unrequited, stingy, and fruitless. Move on from that "love."

Complaining changes nothing. Actions change a lot. Remember, there is a solution to every problem, but not all problems have a simple solution. Some issues are complex and require more time to solve.

Vulnerability is a gift capable of putting you in a vulnerable position. Share that gift wisely.

People can be different behind closed doors. Like Jekyll and Hyde, they're okay one minute, and the next, they aren't. Yet, however scary, one day, you will have to ask yourself: Are you Jekyll or Hyde? And even more frightening, you'll have to answer that question.

If you don't see your worth, they won't either.

Sex can be sex and nothing more.
#relatable

Some come for sex. Some stay for love. While painfully brutal, it's wise to discern the two.

You may be interested in them, but they may not be interested in you. Find a different interest.

Staying together for the kids is a miserable reason to stay together. After all, you can leave the misery without leaving the kids. Co-parent your heart out.

Heartache is heavy. Drowning it with alcohol and dope is heavier. Stay sober, the pain will pass.

People will see your color rather than your potential. Look past those people.

Things are as simple or as complicated as you make them.

We may never be ready. But what is coming will come. Be prepared.

The grass is never greener.

Lies are louder because they bring chaos with them.

Most often, but not always, those with big titles are usually the least qualified.

The lips talk a good game. But good intentions and pure hearts win every time.

Some evils are necessary,
diligently working to show
you the person
you shouldn't be.

We don't run on batteries. It is okay to rest and rejuvenate.

Grief is grueling. Healing is hard. You can get through both.

Most trauma requires trained professionals. Seek counseling when needed.
#mentalhealthmatters

You may have a hard time finding Purpose, but it does exist. Find it. Honor it. Embrace it. Destiny is what you make it.

Feeling like a square peg in a round hole is uncomfortable. But you were meant to be different. So, be bold and stand out anyway.

They will leave you out on purpose, and you will question why. Don't. Just know that your potential will threaten those who doubt theirs.

Intuition is real and always relevant.

If they gossip to you about them, they are talking to them about you. Don't be fooled.

People who gossip about you long to be you. But they can't, although they secretly want to.

Good people are mistreated by those pretending to be good.

Soulmates are said to be a thing, but no one is certain they exist.

Social media is an illusion. Those perfectly curated, filter-fake people in the photos and videos did not wake up like that.
#nofilter

Society is flawed and far from flawless.

There is an upside and a downside to life. Balance is the key.

The world and the people in it will work to harden your heart. Stay soft, yet strong, anyway.

Gaslighting is a narcissist's favorite pastime.

Feeling trapped is just an illusion. Choosing to escape is the hard part.

Everything in life is not black or white; there are gray areas. Coloring outside of the lines is required.

Boxes are made for products, not people. Stop putting yourself in one.

Hurting yourself to hurt others doesn't work.

Selfish people don't give; they take. Stop expecting anything more.

Saying goodbye doesn't feel good. It hurts and hurts and hurts until, eventually, it doesn't hurt anymore.

Faith fades, but a life without faith is a dim-lit life.

God is a mystery; some mysteries aren't meant to be solved.

Money can buy temporary power, but it doesn't mean you're permanently powerful.

Some people are too weak to wear the strength you're asking them to wear. So, stop asking. But don't stop believing.

Walking away from arguments allows you to step into peace.
Do it gracefully.

Parenting is challenging, and giving up and giving in are thoughts. Push through these thoughts.

Just because everyone else likes them does not mean you have to.

Saying no will make a lot of people angry. It's okay. They'll find Glad again.

Just because you like cloudy, rainy days doesn't make you a dark person. You like those days, and that's okay.

Just because everyone else is doing it doesn't mean you have to. Respect your mind and think for yourself.

Being strong is cool. But being soft is cool, too.

True friends will tell you what you need to hear, not what you want to hear.

They hate you because Greatness and Potential love you.

They will respect you behind closed and open doors if they love you.

The energy you feel in the room is genuine. However, the people may not be. Trust your intuition, and don't second-guess yourself.

If it does not feel right, it isn't. Trust your gut.

Negative thoughts don't always mean you are a negative person. If you look on the bright side, they can help you see the situation positively.

It doesn't mean they didn't happen or hurt. But past moments are just that, past moments. Don't bring them into your future.

Some relationships will never connect because staying unhinged is best. Don't force anything, including love.

Being happy alone is where happiness begins.

Side-eye is the weak person's way of saying, "I have a problem."

If their phones are attached to them like another body part, they are hiding something.

Red flags are red, and trying to color them blue makes you feel bluer.

If they're unfaithful and you choose to stay, it's about your lack of confidence and self-respect, not theirs. Know your worth.

It is easier to see the good in others. Make sure to see goodness in yourself, too.

Regret regrets nothing. So, if you're going to do it and have regrets, don't do it. Simple.

You will meet Coward long before you meet Courage. Don't be discouraged; Bravery is a growing pain.

If they are working hard to make you feel unseen, it's because they feel invisible.

Overcomplicating the reality that the ones you love most keep the most secrets changes nothing.

Some lovers play head games because confusion is the only language they know.

Pretending to be naive is not cute; it's reckless.

The lies we tell ourselves are the lies most people tell themselves. At some point, we've got to teach one another the truth.

Being kind to yourself is a rare form of kindness—an unknown cure for life's ill wills and ailments.

Being who you are rather than who they want you to be makes you bolder than 95% of society. Keep being bold.

Closing the book doesn't mean "finale." It means endings end and beginnings begin. Writing a new story with a new beginning and ending is optional.

People treat you how you allow them to treat you. Remember that.

Being used for what you have or can give is not uncommon. It doesn't make it right.

You will have to get up from tables and chairs that no longer serve you. Leave gracefully.

On the way to success, you will want to take everyone with you, but you won't be able to.

Jealousy and envy are things you will feel and face.

They say to focus on the present, but the past will linger, and your human nature will wander. Don't roam too far.

Some days will feel like magic, and other days like misery. Choosing which to feel defines your week.

It's not about how long you have known a person; it is about the health of the connection.

Connections that stand the test of time are genuine, authentic, and sincere.

Trying to prove things to others will prove nothing to yourself.

People can't fill your cup.
If you feel empty, it is
your responsibility to find
fullness and replenish
your own cup.

Anything done in excess becomes excessive, and excessiveness becomes problematic. Moderation is key.

The universe is kind; it grants free warnings. Yet, we see red and say go. We bypass caution lights, ignore wise insights, and head down Therapy Lane—a path we seldom escape. In other words, ignorance is not bliss.

Heartfelt, memorable moments are rare. Cherish them.

Good hearts aren't a dime-a-dozen. Cherish them, too.

You will never be perfect,

and neither will they.

The love and light you seek exist within. It's up to you to see it.

Making decisions while mad is dumb. And anything dumb causes you to make more dumb decisions.

Sharing how you feel rather than holding your feelings in is strength.

Letting go is hard. But once you release, you heal and connect with people, things, and mindsets meant to connect with you.

Time is not on your side.
Make use of time and
wield it wisely.

Both negative and positive energy make an impact—one bringing chaos and the other calm. Choosing which to channel defines your power and the impact it will have.

Smiling through it does not always work. Grit your teeth, open your mouth, and talk it out.

Waiting for perfection will keep you waiting.

Being great is okay; actually, it's better than okay. Don't hide your greatness.

The most significant impact will be the impact you make on yourself.

Starting over is always better than not starting.

Amid heartbreak, ache, and utter confusion, staying true to yourself, your beliefs, and your faith is tough. But, if you stand firm, you won't break.

Growth is uncomfortable, but so is stagnation. Choose one.

A temporary fix

fixes nothing.

Taking accountability for wrong-doings makes things right and makes life worth doing.

Monogamy is a love language. Infidelity is not.

The system pushes anxiety, big pharma pushes pills, and pills push problems. Look up and to nature to find the cure.

You can't stay young forever. After all, growing up happens. Grow with it.

Weak connections disguised as strong connections break— don't relink.

Reacting on the count of your emotions will give you an uncontrollable emotional reaction. Think before you speak.

Laughing is always better than crying. However, a good cry from time to time is refreshing and much-needed.

You will yearn to hear "I love you" from the one you love, and it may not come. But the right "I love you" from your true love will. Have patience.

Embracing vulnerability makes you vulnerable. And it's a beautiful risk. But it's a risk you will have to take.

The dysfunctional environment from childhood does not have to be the environment you stay in or re-create.

Some people only come to conquer and drain your energy. Make sure you recognize those people.

Some friends only stay to find your triggers and push your buttons. Those are not your friends; they are distractions.

Most spirit guides are people actively looking for the Spirit. Don't be fooled.

You will find your tribe when appropriate. You will know your tribe, and your tribe will know you. They will become your soul family.

Your first soaked pillowcase will not be your last. Dry your eyes, change the case, and rest anyway.

True happiness is felt, never forced.

We all get lost with hopes of being found. Sadly, most people don't look for the lost; they cling to the found, leaving you to find yourself.

There will be times when baby steps are the only steps you take. But forward movement, big or small, is still progress.

Your mind is your right and responsibility.

Some people choose to stay sick because healing is too hard.

Some people choose to stay sick because the attention they get from sickness is worth more than the attention they get from healing.

You can't save people that don't want to be saved. Stop trying.

Those closest to you may deny you. The key is not to deny yourself.

Some people refuse to see your greatness because they fear it will conceal theirs. Be great anyway.

The love you give may not be the love you receive. Love anyway but be wise when sharing.

Negative habits don't yield positive results. Positive habits do.

The first war begins within. Be kind to your mind.

Being good to others means nothing if you're not good to yourself.

Holding out hope for hopeless people is a form of captivity—you unchained, and your mind held hostage.

Being a dreamer and a doer are two separate tasks. Do them both.

Manipulation happens when we mistake Insanity for Sanity and Temporary Sense for Stability.

Stressing about tomorrow will not change tomorrow's outcome. Be present today.

Genuine love is not chaotic or traumatic. It's calm and stable.

This is how you will know true love.

Many see kindness as a weak uniform. But it's not about how others see kindness. It's about you and how you choose to wear it.

A clear vision is often cloudy to those not meant to see it.

Jumping off the cliff will cross your mind. Stand still. Stand firm. Think. But don't leap.

Strange can be good sometimes, especially when it transforms the usual into the extraordinary.

Sometimes, we must go first. We can't always wait for others to take the lead.

The person for you is for you, and the things meant for you will be for you.

Narcissists are real, and their abuse is, too.

One day, you may have to be your own hero. Be super. After all, superheroes are good people being super.

Titles mean nothing. Character means everything.

Small minds want you to believe small things. Think big and do big things.

An enlightened person will never brag about being enlightened. Remember that.

Rejection of any kind is protection, but it still hurts.

Listening to silence is one of the best noises you will ever hear.

Dangerous circles
congregate in
"safe" places.

Making peace with past wounds is the only way to heal them—the only way to heal yourself.

Your value has nothing to do with how they define you and everything to do with how you define Yourself.

Holding your breath for too long because you fear failure suffocates potential and kills purpose. Breathe, live, and take the chance.

There will be nooks and crannies that feel like pockets of insanity. They aren't. These moments are temporary fractures in a fractured world.

You are capable if you believe you are capable.

Releasing the hurt you and embracing the healed you will free you.

Every good thing aligns at an appointed time. Forcing the outcome changes destiny—creating a power you can't manage.

Pressing delete will be required. This action includes snakes pretending to be friends, dead-end jobs, and anything else not helping you become your best self.

Life moves on even if you don't move with it—healed, unhealed, not ready. It is still your responsibility to move.

Burdens fill the hearts of those naive enough to put their lives in the hands of others.

Great leaders
lead with compassion,
not with competition.

They will force you to pick a side because not knowing makes them uncomfortable. Choose. Don't choose. It's up to you. Not them.

There's nothing wrong with following a strong leader. There's nothing wrong with being a strong leader, either.

Guilt will hold you hostage and throw away the key. Forgive yourself, release the grief, and live.

Sometimes, it gets worse before it gets better. But it does get better.
Hold on.

The inner critic is the worst critic.

Living vicariously through others is something failures do. Don't be this person, friend, or parent. Create the life you want to live and be happy with it.

Scarcity is a mindset and so is abundance. There is enough to go around. Enough success, enough love, enough wealth. Enough.

Some of the worst cannibals are people you love, trust, and admire. They devour not your flesh but your good heart, kindness—your spirit-filled love.

You have come further than you think but are too close to the situation to see the results. Step back, relax, and don't be overly hard on yourself.

Fear and Self-doubt are acquaintances. They should never become friends.

You will have to talk yourself through difficult conversations and bad situations (possibly alone), but you can and will get through them.

No one is going to heal you but you.

No one is coming to save you but you.

If forgiveness is something you need, remember, you can't forgive others without forgiving yourself first.

Notes to self are random but real moments to write things to yourself that your mouth can't or won't say.

If you ever feel like changing to belong, don't. Stay true to who you are.

Life is messy. But being open and inclined to life's lectures makes living life easier. After all, there is a blessing in every lesson.

Falling is far easier than standing. Get up. Stand up. Stay up.

Many still bleed from the sores of unhealed wounds because they said nothing when they should have said much. Speak up.

Although it should, marriage does not mean monogamy. Choosing to stay faithful does.

People like to assume; they feel it gives them meaning. This poor characteristic holds true for those who feel meaningless.

You need to love yourself enough to say no.

Meekness matters, but most times, life requires the brave to be bold. Not impatient or arrogant or prideful, but bold.

If you don't believe God exists, one day, you will— the fear that hell is real and spending eternity there will eventually convince you.

There is an upside and a downside to life. How you feel on the inside is what matters most.

Feeling accepted, seen, and heard starts with accepting, seeing, and hearing yourself.

Empty promises come from people pretending to be full.

Joy does come in the morning, but it is available any time of the day.

There are more pure hearts than evil hearts in this world. You will think otherwise.

Writing a vision defines destiny, and destiny clears the path. It's up to you to walk it.

The pain you bestow on others is the pain you bestow on yourself.
#karma

If you are upset and it (whatever it is) crosses your mind, don't do it.

No matter how hard life gets, it's your job to do it. No one is going to live for you. After all, people are busy trying their best to live lives they have no idea how to live.

Sometimes things are better left unsaid, and sometimes they aren't. The hard part is deciding when to speak and when to stay quiet.

Looking inward to find what is lost is the best place to look.

Some truths are like shards of glass under our feet—painful when stepped on, yet distinctly beautiful when held up to the light.

You will face loneliness, and you will feel desperate. In this temporary state of yearning, remember, like attracts like. So, don't become desperate for someone desperate. Finding real love takes time.

Pain is part of the process, the cycle of life, and you cannot avoid it. You can, however, handle it.

People conceal problems

they don't want to fix.

Everyone does not love the truth. But the truth loves everyone.

Motivation leaves the room all the time. It's your responsibility to go after it.

Pity parties are not celebrations; no one wants to hear a sob story.

Stop asking, "Why me?" You're not the only one going through what you're going through. So, why not you?

Some of life's best moments happen unexpectedly. Be spontaneous.

Idols are people with problems that you don't see.

Some people are walking burdens—only capable of giving you what they can give themselves. NOTHING.

Devils grant promises they can't keep. They're good at granting misery, though.

Sexual fantasies are seldom true.

They say it drives
men wild and women
bananas. But, when you
peel back the layers of
sex, there is NOT
a penis hard, or a vagina
wet enough to destroy
your life over.

Self-discovery may not lead to a fabulous find. Be prepared to unearth some darkness along the journey.

You have ten fingers, yet finding genuine friends you can count on will take up two. Maybe three.

Every day is what you make it. Stop waiting for others to gift you the joy you seek to find in Yourself.

One day, your friendships will be okay; the next, those you thought had your back will become distant, silent, and disconnected. Let them stay that way. Trust me, sweating stupidity is not worth it.

Losing yourself to gain others is a terrible loss. Be who you are. Love who you are. The right people will come and stay.

You're not placed in a special category called Exempt when it comes to trials, tribulations, and trauma. These pains happen to everyone.

Looking beyond what you see is often the best place to look. Honest answers rest in unseen places.

There's always an opportunity to do better. Making excuses not to is what cowards do.

Letting go and holding on—at some point—you will battle both simultaneously.

Being bold enough to go above the middleman takes you to the top. It's a skill to stay there.

It is better to be okay than not okay. However, society will tell you it's okay not to be okay. This rhetoric is a lie. It's your job to learn that being okay is okay, but getting to a point of being good is better.

Being humble sucks sometimes. But Humbleness kisses you and gently strokes your hair while Ungratefulness stabs you in the back, throws you under the bus, and feeds you to the wolves. Will you be humble? Will you be ungrateful? You must decide.

Looks fade, but an intelligent mind does not. In other words, Vanity is a dog hoping to find a bone, while Intelligence is a mine, never in search of gold. Which would you prefer?

Doing what's right sometimes feels wrong. This feeling will have you questioning your morals, decisions, and truths. Stand firm on the mount of Morality anyway.

We've all broken under the weight of heartache, loss, and tragedy. You will break, too. But, once you consciously decide to heal, stay healed because Broken will stalk you openly and dishonestly. When it does, you will be strong enough to defeat it—openly and honestly.

It is hard to keep going when you have gone and gone and gone and feel you've gotten nowhere. Keep going, anyway. You are going somewhere.

The fairytale is far easier to stomach. Yet, truth, when accepted, is easier to digest.

You're as good as you think you are. If you see yourself as exceptional, then you will be.

Love is not complicated.

People are.

Being brave enough to love the hell out of yourself and others is terrifying. Be bold, brave, and love anyway.

Printed in the USA
CPSIA information can be obtained
at www.ICGtesting.com
CBHW030222270124
3790CB00003B/52